salmonpoetry

Evidence of Freewheeling

TREVOR CONWAY

salmonpoetry

Published in 2015 by
Salmon Poetry
Cliffs of Moher, County Clare, Ireland
Website: www.salmonpoetry.com
Email: info@salmonpoetry.com

Copyright © Trevor Conway, 2015

ISBN 978-1-910669-23-5

All rights reserved. No part of this publication may be reproduced or transmitted in any form or by any means, electronic or mechanical, including photography, recording, or any information storage or retrieval system, without permission in writing from the publisher. The book is sold subject to the condition that it shall not, by way of trade or otherwise, be lent, resold or otherwise circulated without the publisher's prior consent in any form of binding or cover other than that in which it is published and without a similar condition, including this condition, being imposed on the subsequent purchaser.

COVER IMAGE: *Steven Pearse Conway*
COVER DESIGN & TYPESETTING: *Siobhán Hutson*
Printed in Ireland by Sprint Print

*Salmon Poetry gratefully acknowledges the support of
The Arts Council / An Chomhairle Ealaoín*

Acknowledgements

I'd like to acknowledge the following publications for printing some of these poems: *Poetry Salzburg Review, Cuadrivio, Periodico de Poesia, Inclement, ROPES, The Galway Review, FUSION, The Artistic Atlas of Galway, Decanto, Read This, The Sharp Review, Poetic Expressions, Flash Magazine, The Gown* and *Over the Edge – The First Ten Years.*

Thanks to Jessie Lendennie and Siobhán Hutson of Salmon, for their work with me on this book. Thanks also to James Harrold, Galway City Arts Officer, and Galway City Council, for the bursary I received, and their general support for the arts.

Thanks to all who were generous enough to give me feedback many years ago, when I really needed it, to steer me away from writing very bad poetry, including Edward Nee, Frank L Ludwig, Catherine Wylie and Dermot Healy.

My appreciation goes to Val Nolan in particular, for very precise, honest and astute comments in a poetry workshop class I did as part of an undergrad arts degree. Many thanks to all the others in that class, and to all of the NUIG MA in Writing 2009/10 class, for feedback and friendship. Same goes for all on Splinter4All, Writing4All, Poetry Ireland Forum and The Poetry Forum.

I'd like to give a special mention to John Mc Loughlin, my secondary school English teacher in Summerhill College, Sligo, whose teaching of poetry was probably responsible for my initial interest in reading and writing poems.

Thanks to Kevin Higgins and Sarah Clancy for advice, and appreciation to both Kevin and Susan Millar DuMars for all the good work they do for new writers. Thanks also to the various members of Galway Arts Centre classes for their valuable feedback.

To Conor Lynch and Darren Prendergast, thanks for encouragement, feedback and friendship.

Love and appreciation to my parents, for their constant support, lack of pressure and, of course, regular dinners. Ditto to my bros and sis, Karl, Enda, Steeboy and Elaine, for encouragement and feedback on my work, but mostly for fulfilling relationships and constant abuse.

Special thanks to Sandra, for feedback, support, entertainment and eccentric vocabulary, and especially for making the days richer.

I'd like to dedicate this book to Freda Conway, someone I admire.

CONTENTS

Ivy	11
Black and White	12
Threads	13
Canines at the Ready	14
The Taste of Raspberries	16
Hemispheres	17
Supper at Emmaus	18
Sunday	19
Fasciola Hepatica	20
Dust	22
Garavogue	23
Nothing Like a Death	24
Enlightenment	25
Overlooking Galway	26
Owl	27
Define Me	28
Second Glance	30
Running	32
Connected	33
Father and Son in the Pub	38
Timofte Against Bonner	39
All Earth's Creatures	40
Passing the Test	41
Trimester	43
Abandoned	44
Relativity	46

Bedside	47
Forecast	48
Afterwards	50
Final Draft	51
Similarity	52
Lisbon Hostel	53
The Drunken Poet Speaks Out	54
The White Line	55
Words and Days	56
Winterlude	57
Evolution by Committee	58
April	61
Inspired	63

Ivy

A family's monument
Half-bearded
With fluttering scales,
Its cut cement

Your crutch,
Go, creep over
Its rough skin,
Gather in heaps

At gable edges
And flail your rage
Toward the sky,
Craving its fire.

Cling to the heel
Of spreading concrete,
Like a warrior unable
To accept defeat.

You will wrap
Round each edge,
Cast your veins
On newer ground,

Obscure the touch
Of human hands –
Not consume,
But embrace.

Black and White

I stared at the screen:
It was "black and white",
Or, as I called it,
"Grey".
(I was a pedantic child.)

My parents said they were old films,
Images from long ago,
So, naturally, I assumed everything
Was black and white:
The trees,
The clothes,
The sky
And skin.
What an amazing world.

When did it change? I wondered.
Did everyone just wake up
And find themselves in colour?

Nothing is black and white now.
But I want to believe again.
I want to see the world in these two shades.

The orange street lamp glows
As evening ripens blue.
Words fall to the page:
Black and white.

Threads

Like a hunchback on the floor,
Its shadow thinned by candlelight,
Faded jeans and jumpers fly,
Adding to its sloping height.

Each item wears its time of year,
From airy summer to winter-weight.
A flailing shirt falls to the floor,
Arms at the angle of ten-to-eight.

Stripes of blue and white emerge,
Print peeling from the chest,
A freckled face fills its hole,
Lips and hair once caressed.

Worn, but worn for something more
Than warmth, allegiance or style;
Memories and emotions woven in,
For now, it belongs to no pile.

I see character in all things worn:
The wire hanger bent out of shape,
The candle's wick drowning in wax,
The cotton neck's oval gape.

Those stripes still hang to the edge of a chair
As the hunchback is cleared away,
But every fabric sheds its skin.
Loosened threads will always stay.

Canines at the Ready

Creeping
Slowly,
Staring
Intensely,

Stepping,

Stopping,

Stepping.

You
Chew,
I
Am riveted,
Cloaked
In the silence
Of camouflage.

I value you in protein,
Lust
For your flesh –
It is my right
To take you.

Stepping,

Stopping,

Stepping.

Still oblivious,
Still chewing,
Unlistening.

I
Come closer,
Ready
To strike.

I pounce,
Wrestle,
Open my mouth –
There's daggers in my smile.

Welcome
To
My body.

The Taste of Raspberries

I bit into a peach,
And somehow, the sour kick
Of flesh softened by four days' waiting
Reminded me of raspberries,
Dunally raspberries,
Skulking behind the fir trees of my childhood home.

We'd pinch them off like eggs from a nest,
Be on our way
Across the rocky stream dipping and tumbling to Sligo town,
Or whipped by low twigs
As we scurried between trees,
A burst football or two
Kicked to the base of each trunk.
Sometimes, kids from fields away
Would come to play
(Or cousins, measured in roads).
They'd steal a berry or two.

Today, I'll buy my fruit in the Galway market,
Sure to pluck a Sligo face
Shining between the shoulders and scarves.
Here is where they come some Saturdays.

I'll cross the Corrib,
Atlantic spray webbed to my window.
I play in Salthill, too,
But I've never found a raspberry
At the bottom of the ocean.

Hemispheres

A face of sand
Far from the fire of the sun –
That will be my face,
Flat as lake ice,
Bound in chains
Held by the brain's impulse.
I will be a reptile,
Flaunt my indifference,
Glad to feel no degree of joy.

What could I make
Without that fiery flush –
A page of morning snow?
Symbolic shapes are struck
Beyond a creasing face,
But stories are revealed in eyes.
Paintings, poems, all their kind,
Scream of joy and despair
Like jagged, weeping women.

Smouldering words,
Colours branded on canvas –
How far can they fulfil?
Shadows fall on them,
The shape of a child,
Each artist a puppeteer.
Parents know
We are burnt with both:
We neither melt nor drown.

Supper at Emmaus
After Caravaggio

Come,
Step closer to my falling light,
My dark edges,
Where a pilgrim's hand extends
And ruffled sleeves invite crooked lines of shadow,
Thick curls of brown hair.

Jesus,
Wearing the face of a youth,
Blesses the bread, the chicken and fruit,
With eyes lowered,
Fingers curved toward his palm.
And they realise:

Their crucified master,
Here in an unfamiliar form
To share their supper,
His plump, beardless face
No longer gaunt and frail.

Their arms and elbows flung out,
Fingers pressed into the ribs of a chair,
They form a ring
From which their host
Is removed.

But you may come,
Reach for the hanging berries,
Step closer
To my falling light,
My dark edges.

Sunday

Coffee and scones
On a Sunday morning:
The bumble bee hum of a lawnmower
Frees the scent of cut grass
As light screams from the sun.
In the shade,
Pages spread,
Magazines flung to the corner
Like ruffled orphans.
Indented butter
Crowns the soft bread,
A coffee ring
On page seven.

Fasciola Hepatica

You are born into faeces
On dew-laden grass,
Emerge from your egg
At ten degrees,
Crawl
Through bending blades
Till water sings like a siren.

By a rock,
A constellation of frog spawn.
The flow is cold and fast.
Hours of swirling, searching:
Survival grows dimmer.

The humped back of a snail,
Your spine
Penetrates its soft flesh.
You feed as it feeds,
Live through its life.

Hairs loosen.
Cells change.
Larvae form within you.
A tail whips
As you burrow free from the carcass.
The empty shell,
Lined with rotting flesh,
Drifts with the current.

A green path
Tips through the water.
From blade to soggy blade,
You struggle on.
Each passing animal
Could be your survival.
A muck-coated leg
Plunges into the soil,
And passes on.

The grass grows dry,
And you suffer.

Evening closes,
Offering dew.
Warm breath
Passes over you,
The crunch of jaws
Around you – taken into the mouth
With a clump of wet grass.

On you move,
Over the tongue,
Until you reach the liver.

Fattening,
Attached to the bile duct,
You are where you belong.

Dust

A stiff drawer
Coated in time,
Searching for something recalled,

A withered image
Comes to hand:
A face I've never seen,

Though I've known it
Through my life
As an older, paler thing.

Where are the wandering lines
That spread across your face,
The puffed cheeks, sagging neck,
Thin, dreaming eyes?

There's hope in this face,
A gaze firm with ideals,
Sepia skin, rounded cheeks,
Hair full as a cloud.

Move your pouting lips
And whisper
What expectations charmed your thoughts,
And how they were chased from view.

Maybe you saw a sloping roof,
A table heavy with plates and hands,
Heads you thought would never pale –
Or the fist of the man you loved.

I wipe the image clean,
Knowing dust will come again
Like dark snow falling.

Am I so mad to dream?
My tired eyes are opened wide.
Dust, come settle on me.

Garavogue

Roaring, splashing, frothing, bending,
Invading every hollow,
Rushing as people bustle
With bags and brief hellos,
Your body is a writhing thing,
Reshaping with your flow.
By Stephen Street, below the bridge,
You surge toward the sea,
My face reflected on your dark skin
While bankers and mothers hurry.
This town has changed, but you remain,
With all your careless beauty.

Nothing Like a Death

There's nothing like a death
To bring in a crowd:
A slow-stepping wave of sorrow,
Sober faces, solemn words,
Whispers at the fringe.

Lichen-spotted stone
Stands in congregation
As careless steps
Collect a skirt of mud,
A deep impression in dirt.

The coffin drops,
The body consumed
Slowly,
Painfully.
The shovel grunts
As the fact is nailed home.

And with a blessing,
All are scattered;
The squawk of a crow
Stark as a bell.
The count of heads
Has measured the person,
As wheels turn on gravel.

There's nothing like a death
To bring in a crowd.
Death's tragedy
Is greater than life's
Familiarity.

Enlightenment

The thin flame flickers
As he scribbles,
A silent player
In humanity's finest,
Humblest moment,
The room's dim corners
Like doubts creeping in.

He bends his neck
To see better
The words he's written.
His beard tips the table,
Obscuring the phrase
"Natural selection".

Beads of sweat trickle down,
And he knows it is good.

Overlooking Galway

The tiptoe of rain
Tapping as we huddle
Under the black umbrella.

Curves: your cheek,
Tongue between your teeth.
Town melts into empty fields.

Amber lights
Like distant fires.
A swallow gorges arcs of air.

I see its flight
In the brown of your eyes,
And contemplate a different life.

Country's charm,
Spread in evening haze,
Draws me away.

Charged fingertips
Brush curls from your temple,
Around your ear.

Owl

Are you a statue, perched so nobly
Like a king who rules by fear,
Discreet wings fluttering only
To catch your prey unaware?

Your stony face shows no feeling,
Observing from a steady height,
The deep reach of your call revealing
The hidden heartbeat of the night.

Distant stars gather to view,
Like beaded Roman nobility,
The ancient task, each night a new
Alchemy of nature's currency.

Sailing through the summer night
In silent flight, like a breath,
You swoop, delivering with your bite
A piece of life, shrieking death.

The heartbeat's still, no fleshy sound
Until you fly to your lofty throne,
Claiming your right to the priceless pound
Before the day's first light is thrown.

When these fields are loud and bright,
You'll claim no right to an earthly fee,
But darkness comes, and another flight:
Some night, I know, you'll come for me.

Define Me

What kind of impression do you make
When you walk into a room?
How many faces turn and linger?

Does it really matter?

What clothes do you wear?
What do they reveal,
Suggest
Or conceal?

Whether I'm cold or warm,
Daring or shy,
Or that I favour a certain style.

What about your name?

A name is not a choice.

But those who surround you
Shape you.
Where are you from?
What colour is your skin?

A different colour
In autumn, winter,
Spring and summer.

How much do you earn?
What do you drive?
Describe your home.

I earn enough to survive.

I can define you
By the passions consuming you:
The films you see, the books you read,
The tunes swirling round you.

If you can define by variety.

Turn the light on, please.

Second Glance

It's strange to like a face,
To appreciate its curves and lines,
Humps and hollows,
The twisted arch of the jaw.

Our words and deeds
Define,
Defame
Or distinguish,
But we pay for skin
That will crack and smudge.

Fertile hair is coiled
With the vigour of the young.
Does it spring, too,
From the shape of the face?

Silver might be richer
From one town to another,
Slung around the necks of tribal women.

What hangs will sway.
What's dabbed will change our eyes
As much as the light.

If you are a woman,
I will judge your beauty
Before your words.
Will you afford me the same?

I have wanted a different face,
Something
Better.
But how, then, would my thinking change?

I have pitied others
I shouldn't have.

Social value, we know, is a surface measure,
Every layer of fat a Jewish star.
I once heard a passing remark:
"Shoot me if I ever let myself go that far."
The unfit are prey,
Attracting the predator,
So stay away!

Beauty, a kind of gravity
Drawing us closer.
I strive to make the prettiest words —
Words to attract who?

Running

Where grass grows, I will run –
A swift gazelle as I heave.
So fit, healthy and young,
In the flush of flight I believe
Life is physical, nothing more,
Flowing through every muscle and pore.
The brain can express or explore,
But what will it achieve?

The sun goes down like a dying beast,
Nature's laws wrapped round its throat.
All the heady young compete,
With little time to devote.
A page is a field for old men,
Where I will run a dripping pen,
Ideas rounding again and again
As I sit and dote.

Connected

She sees many things:
Windows in a whirl of colour,
Pictures, actions, numbers, words.
She sees a multitude,
And knows their status,
The business of their lives,
Her place apart
Among them.

Still, she searches.
A picture, some quality it has
– Maybe the humour of the light –
Takes her to a sunny weekend
Lying on a Turkish beach.

I wonder what he's doing now –
Likely looking in the mirror.

Eyeing tanned legs emerging from a girl's green dress,
She considers her next trip:
Stockholm? Singapore?
Maybe Syracuse.

He was reading that novel,
1984,
Said it was the best book he ever read,
Telling me all about it:
People were leaping up and down
In their places
And shouting at the tops of their voices.
The Two Minutes Hate.

Tapping, constant tapping
Like an endless echo applauding
Through captured fragments of conversations,
Music slips through an open window.

A sound like a crying child,
Familiar:
Just her ring-tone,
Wailing.

"Hey, Mum, how are things?"

They talk of trivial matters,
Like a train stopping
On the way to a bigger town,
Dissecting the lives of others:
Her sister's cursing child,
A neighbour's ill health,
Four students killed in a car crash.

As words tumble out, her thoughts diverge:
This could be the last time I talk to you.
Who knows what could happen tomorrow.
And I haven't even said sorry.

"I bought a new thing for the computer,"
Her mother says,
"But I can't get it to work.
Maybe you could help me with it."

Why can't I just say it?

"I'm pretty busy for the next few weeks,
But sure, Mum – no problem."

I'm sorry.

Like water trickling over toes,
Rising foam above her knees,
A dull pride swells inside her:
Modern life a better life
Than all the lives lived before.
But, for all the interactions,
The easy words splattered and borrowed,

All the voices sounding separate notes,
Life seems, at times, a soliloquy.

As her mother's voice dies
With a husky cough
And "Bye, love. Bye",
She looks around and wonders:
Is there anything else to search for?

Moving away from what she sought,
Coming close to what she needs,
She feels she's always searching,
Her world expanding silently
With hidden scaffolds and cranes,
Silent workers
Across the globe,
Building in secret.
She sees pages
Sliding out of every window,
Rippling in the wind, drifting
Through the fumes,
Between wires,
Torn on the tips of road signs,
Over cliffs, above the sea,
Pushed along like wandering birds.
Dipping under a bridge, they rise
Above the jagged teeth of Sydney Opera House,
Floating through open windows
Ten floors up.

Her path is blocked.
She pushes and prods,
Afraid to stop,
Sees another window,
Full of books, alluring titles,
Covers designed to intrigue.
She looks inside,
Hears whispering voices from every age,
Every corner and spine,

Tasting lines and curves,
Dots and spaces,
Separate sounds
Embracing to represent
Others' thoughts,
Savouring the swell
As she moves down the page:

"I will wake one day and walk away
Through fields beyond the touch of hands.
Concrete huddled at a distance,
My city lights will shine above.
I'll tread on snapping twigs,
On yielding moss
That sheds its load.
The world will speak in steps and calls,
Time measured in shades of blue.
Hair will scale down my back.
I'll wipe myself with grass,
The curve of my jaw disappearing
Like a rock beneath the undergrowth.
Food will run, jump
Or seek the sun,
No traffic light to clip my flight.
I will read no book, play no guitar.
I will not be online, not be aware
Of the latest trends.
My needs will not be measured
In coin or paper.
I'll see no pretty face,
But I'll see poetry everywhere."

She looks around,
And all she's known is a shuddering shadow
Thrown against the wall of a cave.
All her life, she's been chained,
Unable to see the flames.

Now the path is clear,
She resumes her search,
But, in a moment, reflects:
What's missing from my life?
I'm interesting,
Attractive.
I have lots of friends.
There's nothing wrong
With the way I live.

We all deserve a stage,
A bedroom press
To publish our thoughts.
We are the age of the individual
Attached.

Two minutes hate.

Two minutes love.

I'm happy.

One message received
Offers bigger breasts,
But she's found what she wants.
Prompted, she enters a string of digits,
Details that say so little,
And clicks to pay.

Another window offers discussion.
So many things
– The same faces and half-names,
Its daily furniture –
Feel, to her, like a café.

She closes the window,
Slams down the screen
And unfurls the bed clothes.

She is offline.

Father and Son in the Pub

His arm, arched over my head,
Ushers me through the wooden door.
I scan the lit faces
Of middle-aged men who throw glances.
Mounting a stool by the bar,
I'm a king on my throne.

Two glasses before us,
The inequality so brazen.
I fight the temptation,
But it drains to a puddle,
Paler in its paucity,
His glass a statue with barely a chip taken.

Darting looks, heavy breaths, revised posture –
None convince him to drink faster
As he mixes words with the other men.
A slap on the bar
From the man with the red face
Kicks off a round of laughter,
But I don't get their humour.

While my father's back is turned, I steal a taste.
He sees me, but ignores the fact.
I stare at the white strands framing his face,
The curious shape of his stubble,
The froth hanging on his lip.

I want to have that power.

And now I do:
I've tasted the salmon,
Rotten with knowledge.
There's froth on my face.
I don't know how it got there,
Can't even remember the taste.

Timofte Against Bonner

He walks up,
Places the ball,
Approaches slow
As a timid antelope.

The hunched man in grey
Follows the trail of his eyes,
The turn of his hips.
Green and golden tides
Await.

Timofte strikes —
His posture
Betrays.

Bonner saves.

All Earth's Creatures

A cloud of midges mingles
Through summer evening light
As bodies throng the church door
To smell blood in wine
And taste the body of Christ.

The statue of Mary hides
A slender, stalking cat
Eyeing the wings of a crow
With a kind of slow, silent
Devotion to its task,

Worshipping, too, in a way,
Like every living thing:
One creed in common
Through the turns of summer
To autumn, winter and spring,

All Earth's creatures Pagan,
In every thing they do,
Eating, drinking, or mating,
Every day of their lives,
Worth a prayer or two.

Flying, walking or swimming,
Striving to live and kill
In the name of nothing but life,
With no moral pause,
Each with unique skill,

Nature practised in puddles,
In the hop and chirp of birds,
And *homo sapiens*, despite
Its systems of belief,
Prays like any herd.

Passing the Test

I've labelled the symbols,
Identified the parts.
The key twists, gear shifts to first.

"Take a left," he mutters,
And I move off,
Indicating my intention,

Into the fickle world of the road,
Where my skills are public,
My flaws gigantic.

Sliding fingers, springy legs,
I read the wheels and lights, the shape
Of others' aims,

Tracing the focus of vision,
Judging speed and distance,
In search of fifth gear.

A motorbike passes
Like a three-minute rock tune;
A truck before me, vast as a novel.

Some who pass
Are barely able,
Though no road is built for tests.

I'll merge into the mass,
Fling myself from every roundabout,
Cruising into the sun.

Momentum will come in time,
Following from patience,
Awareness.

Back to where we began,
I have too much faith
In one man's evaluation.

I wait for the words
Till he flips the page and says,
"Well done."

Trimester

All I know is darkness,
Starved of any sight.
I take the blood of another,
Though uninclined to fight.
No morals or opinions
Have rendered me polite.

I could be a father,
Or I could be a priest.
I could be a gambler.
I could also be a thief.

Suspended in this liquid,
A fish pacified,
The silence between the beats
Reveals the world outside.
My fate is on the wind,
Though others may be my guide.

I could teach your children,
Deliver bags of coal
Or live a carefree life
Surviving on the dole.

I could lead a country
Or save a stranger's life.
I could be your lover.
I could even rape your wife.

If you had that knowledge
As your womb's lining grew,
Would you deem my life so precious
Or erase its residue?
Mother, father, love me
Despite the things I'll do.

Abandoned

A pale face emerges from the night,
Like snow-melt at the edge of a log.
Smooth, shallow cheeks,
Hair sprung with curls,
Her clothes are torn,
Worn, holes
And threads.

Thin arms reach out
And drop, trembling, past her hips.
On the air,
The salt of the sea rises
And spreads.

I ask her name.
The green rings of her eyes turn down.
Her lips quiver,
Skin moistened
With cold, heavy rain.
And still I wait for the sound.

Her mouth is unmoved,
But I hear the voice,
Fading to a cadence like an old photo's edge:
"My tongue has been cut,
But I'll weave a tapestry of words."
I ask where she's from,
And she falls,
Pressing her finger
Into the mucky ground.

The shape she cuts is strange,
Though familiar,
A ragged edge
Of teeth and tongues.
Her fingerprint lingers on the dirt

Till a wave of water washes over.
"I'm lost,
Abandoned.
All six of my children are dead," I hear.
And she warms my lips with a kiss.

Her eyelids flicker
As raindrops dance hard through puddles.
In their murky water,
She struggles to see her own image.
"The sea is silent.
No-one will come to save me," I hear.
I open my mouth,
Ready to offer softer words,
But she doesn't understand,
And flowing between us,
There's a dark,
Thickening mist.

Relativity

Opinions are the crudest things,
Delivered like a trumpet solo
Out of time.
They come in clusters,
Defined by their neighbours.

Saturn's moons
Follow like besotted suitors:
Push them gently –
They'd follow Jupiter
Instead.

Earth was flat
Till inflated by science,
Fat as a Renaissance priest.
Its flatness grew
From the dream of fullness.

Sonnets, songs and painted scenes
Are fashioned from comparison,
Analogy their core –
The flare of a tail
Miles from the sun.

Can you measure any thing
In a vacuum?
These lines could be eclipsed
By Whitman, Frost or Poe,
Or your nearest neighbour.

Bedside

The crease of your spine,
A thin thread
Of knowledge gained:
Some measure of satisfaction.
I feel your years in weeks,
Your space in the world
Swelling in mind.
In the lamplight,
You slouch to a stupor,
Throwing your earthy smell my way.
Your sharp edges now smooth,
I have conquered you.

Forecast

Beyond the window,
A rage of wind and rain.
A church bell hums
Over the slow procession.
Black fabric ripples,
Hats pinned by rigid hands.

I see the shine of wet shoes
As careless feet splash through puddles,
And far above it all:
The twisted tip of a cloud
Dipped in yellow light.

What kind of sky
Will usher me from the world?
A brooding autumn,
Leaves scraping pirouettes
Over kerbs and windows,
Fainting with each lull?

A blue-lit morning?
The gloomy, grey horizon of December?
It might be the heart
Of a Sunday afternoon,
Newspaper spread like a mat
On coffee-scented air,

Or a summer evening
Taken to raw pink,
Where birds perch
In statues of silhouette
And night rolls in slow
As a tired dream,

A day of wind
Pitched at the sting of a face,
Or a still morning
At January's end,
Sunlight glaring,
Frost in the shade.

I wish, one day,
Bells would hold their tongues –
The height of summer,
Sun set in the sky
Like a jewel, and every face
As still as a framed portrait,

Or to decide
The day, the time, the place,
And whether it comes
Like hail or snow.

By a window,
A curled cat sleeps
As legs and arms
Bustle through sunshine.
I gaze at the changing sky:
No day will do.

Afterwards

Emotions like tides
Coming back for a taste,
Images of you
In far-off places.
Curls still creep across your face,
I'm sure,
And I'm sorry.
So different in ways,
Though less in emotion.
And who's to say
There's a measure on feeling?

Final Draft

In a long, bright, cluttered room,
This man has made his second home,
Where tools and thoughts fill the shelves,
Goaded each day to twist and roam.

The smell is of nature prostituted,
Damp and stale, of things shaped well.
He trims a little off the cheek,
Pinches the brow to a subtle swell.

His cupped palm reshapes the skull.
His thumb bends the crooked nose.
A head shaped through the years,
Each day, it reforms and grows.

He finds fault in familiarity,
A kind of distance, where every flaw
Grows like a tumour and clarity comes
Through little failures, the closer he draws,

Like a body's cells, which die and change
Though the person's quite the same.
But bodies wither where words flourish,
And stone can carry a name.

The artist's mind is a restless thing,
Each light, a new cud to chew.
Even in sleep, his knuckles twitch,
Ready to do or undo.

And in my room, a drawer leaks,
Where all my poems are wet.
One day, they'll be dry and hard –
The final draft is death.

Similarity

Those who have shared
Many passing years
Often bear a close resemblance,
It's said.
I see its proof,
Sifting through my parents' generation,

Rapport sculpted on cheeks,
A story told
Like two pages of one book,
As though emotions shared
Are stored in the rising, dipping
Landscape of muscle.

My face may rise in tandem,
Might play the slow duet
Into the years.
It may carve its own path,
Like chiselled ivory in the moon's light.

There are mountains and valleys
In my face.

Lisbon Hostel

Orange juice gurgles into a glass.
The toaster throws up tanned slices
Like a one-jump trampoline.

Sandra presses her thumb
Into a plump satsuma
Till its skin yields.
The flesh parts in segments,
Passes between her lips.

Two girls enter,
Speaking their hieroglyphics.
The fridge opens.
Sandra whispers:
"They better not steal our milk."

One takes a tub of butter.
The other leafs through a brown loaf.
I bring the toast to the table,
Leaving two slices of bread nearby
To stake our claim.

The kettle rumbles.
Juice seeps from Sandra's lips.

The Drunken Poet Speaks Out

There's no place for poets like me.
To write your verses elegantly
Means to take a humble tone,
Fascinated by theme alone.

Experience gives all your weight,
No room for the abstract or the ornate.
Rhyme's assigned to the frivolous poem,
Scorned, and weighed as light as foam.

These words will never reach your eyes,
Whether they might be foolish or wise,
So raise your glass and drink to me:
My words are words you'll never see.

The White Line

He hangs in the air,
Arms outstretched –
A brief tableau
Contesting the ball.
It rolls free,
From foot to hand,
Held at the mercy
Of a shaped leg.
He throws himself,
Slowed by scars
Of age and injury,
The sting on his hand
The most beautiful pain.
A desperate lunge,
He wraps his palms
Around its curve,
Takes a fist to the ribs,
Struggling to stand
Through the flurry of legs and hands.

His name echoed
In men's voices,
He hears the sideline pleas,
Heavy breaths behind
As he charges free
From the stampede.
He sees the soaring posts
Just beyond his range,
Gains a few steps,
Free arm fending off
Unwanted attention.
He twists his body,
Makes the kick before
He's dragged to ground
Like prey, heaving,
Studs into his knee.
Blood shines through the muck
As the ball hangs, arcs
Over the bar.

Words and Days

The measured lines of a poem
Mock designs for life:
So much time to perfect a phrase,
And words are so precise.
If life was an art,
How refined could it be?
And doesn't half its joy lie with uncertainty?
Lives will always come to words,
Which breathe their legacy.

Winterlude

Mist hangs thick in winter air,
Blooms of breath from mouth and nose.
Ice defines the crease of clothes,
Trees cut brown and bare.

Water flows, cold and clear.
Branches bear the weight of rain,
Their winking drops a shiny mane.
Such stillness in the air.

Ashen skies deprived of light
Threaten their load on soggy ground.
The noise of the world's a whispering sound,
So slow, so hollow and slight.

Sickly blades of frosted grass
Crunch below unsteady feet,
But soon, these images retreat;
Each season will come and pass.

Evolution by Committee

Remember that idea I had?
Lungs.

You also suggested the four-assed elephant.

`What's our ethos again?`

Survival.

How about a flower
With the scent of a female bee?
And hey, why not its appearance, too?

What would be the point of that?

To pass on its pollen
Without producing nectar.

Crazy.
But I like it.

`Here's my idea:`
`A rat with wings.`

How original.

We've done that already.

`What do you mean?`

The bat.

I have a much better idea:
A rat with bristling hairs
Tipped with venom.

Yes, I can see it:
A little ball of tightening muscle,
The hairs standing firmer,
Clear droplets forming,
Deterring any predator.

Enough!

All my ideas,
They're so avant-garde.
Remember the eye?
The octopus?
Who else could've fashioned feathers
From scales?

We've all had good ideas.

`Not you — you're boring.`

When I came up with sexual reproduction,
You were all interested.

True.

`What started this off?`

I don't know.

It doesn't matter.

```
How about a creature
Completely hairless,
Living in a cold climate?
```

Ridiculous.

```
But wait:
It has the ability
To take the hair of another species
And put it over itself.
Its vision is weak, but —
```

It finds a way to improve it?

```
Yes.
```

Brilliant!
But maybe it could have *some* hair.

```
Maybe.
```

What other ridiculous traits would it have?

```
It's not ridiculous.
```

**Stop!
Next issue:
Any ideas for the winter season?**

```
Fur.
```

April
In memory of Pearse Devins
(1958-1967)

February crawls.
March stands up.
April moves at a jog.

I hardly remember the white breath of winter,
Waking each day as vigorous as a river.
There's always been a sadness in my mother,
This time of year,
Days like these
Seen through wistful eyes.
I never realised why
Till now:

It was a day like this
Pearse died.
I've seen his face in pictures,
The uneven sweep of his curls,
The charming grin
Of a nine-year-old boy.

The football rolled
Across the road.
He followed.

Mum became the youngest child.

She never let us play out the front,
Said it was for the flowers.
But I knew what blooms she sought to protect.
By curling balls and bending legs on sunny days,
We brothers fought and loved.
Flat balls still litter the edge,
Orange bladders like open wounds.

Pearse would be a man now,
Too old for games,
His curls withered,
Chin stubbled,
Driving to Ballyshannon.

Mum sometimes kicks the ball.
She smiles, though her chin hangs low.
When I kick the ball in April,
It goes faster than any car.

Inspired

All the best ideas
Are conceived at ease.
I've written sonnets over coffee,
Drifting with its aroma
From face to glancing face,
Or sitting on a rock,
Its mossy coat foam-tipped,
As a river whispers.
Stories have emerged
By fire and TV.
At half-time,
I penned a lament:
Milan 3 – Liverpool nil.
A blank book lies by my bed.
By morning, the sheets are filled.

From falling apples,
Great theories have formed.
Idle hours at a patent office
Cast revealing light,
A king's dilemma solved
In the steam of a public bath.

I have no great theory,
Just words,
Like an old friend returning
In new clothes.

Some day,
I'll sit with paper by my side,
A strain on my face
As I reach for the pen,
To set the seeds
Of the Great Irish Novel.
Word will tumble on word,
Each letter a stamp of gold,
The touch of fire in my blood.

Then, I will flush.

Photograph by Steven Pearse Conway

TREVOR CONWAY, from Sligo, writes poetry, fiction and songs, as well as book reviews, drama and film scripts. An album of his songs has been recorded and released, titled *Morning Zoo*. He has an MA in Writing from NUI Galway, and has been a featured reader at events such as Galway's Over the Edge series, the Tuam Arts Festival and Cork's O Bhéal series. His work has appeared in magazines and anthologies in Ireland, Austria, the UK, the US, India and Mexico, where his poems have been translated into Spanish.

www.trevorconway.weebly.com